THE PRAYER OF
MARY AND THE SAINTS

Sr. Catherine Aubin, O.P.

Preface by Pope Francis

NOTES ON PRAYER
Volume 7

Our Sunday Visitor
Huntington, Indiana

Copyright © Dicastery for Evangelization 2024
Palazzo San Pio X, Via della Conciliazione, 5 00120 Città del
Vaticano
www.pcpne.va; www.iubilaeum2025.va
Published 2024 by Our Sunday Visitor, Inc.

Our Sunday Visitor Publishing Division
Our Sunday Visitor, Inc.
200 Noll Plaza
Huntington, IN 46750
1-800-348-2440

ISBN: 978-1-63966-280-7 (Inventory No. T2942)
eISBN: 978-1-63966-281-4
LCCN: 2024948665

Cover and interior design: Amanda Falk
Cover art: Adobestock

OSV extends thanks to the Catholc Truth Society for its collaboration
in producing this book.

Printed in the United States of America

Contents

Preface by Pope Francis

———

Prayer is the breath of faith, its most proper expression. It's like a silent cry that comes out from the heart of whoever trusts and believes in God. It's not easy to find words to express this mystery. How many definitions of prayer we can gather from the saints and masters of spirituality, as well as from the reflections of theologians! Nevertheless, it is always and only in the simplicity of those who live prayer that prayer finds expression. The Lord, moreover, warned us that, when we pray, we must not waste words, deluding ourselves that thus we will be heard. He taught us rather to prefer silence and to entrust ourselves to the Father, who knows the kind of things we need even before we ask for them (see Mt 6:7–8).

The Ordinary Jubilee of 2025 is already at the door. How to prepare ourselves for this event, so important for the life of the Church, if not by means of prayer? The year 2023 was set aside for a rediscovery of the conciliar teachings, contained especially in the four constitutions of the Second Vatican Council. It is a way of keeping alive the mandate that the Fathers gathered at the council wished to place in our hands, so that by means of its implementation, the Church might recover its youthful face and proclaim, in a language adapted to the men and women of our time, the beauty of the Faith.

Now is the time to prepare for a year that will be dedicated entirely to prayer. In our own time the need is being felt more and more strongly for a true spirituality capable of responding to the great questions which confront us every day of our lives, questions caused by a global scenario that is far from serene. The ecological-economic-social crisis aggravated by the recent pandemic; wars, especially the one in Ukraine, which sow death, destruction, and poverty; the culture of indifference and waste that tends to stifle aspirations for peace and solidarity and keeps God at the margins of personal and social life. ... These phenomena combine to bring about a ponderous atmosphere that holds many people back from living with joy and serenity. What we need, therefore, is that our prayer should rise up with greater insistence to the Father so that he will listen to the voice of those who turn to him, confident of being heard.

This year dedicated to prayer is in no way intended to affect the initiatives which every particular Church considers it must plan for in its own daily pastoral commitment. On the contrary, it aims to recall the foundation on which the various pastoral plans should be developed and find consistency. This is a time when, as individuals or communities, we can rediscover the joy of praying in a variety of forms and expressions. A time of consequence enabling us to increase the certainty of our faith and trust in the intercession of the Virgin Mary and the saints. In short, a year in which we can have the experience almost of a "school of prayer," without taking anything for granted (or at cut-rate), especially with regard to our way of praying, but making our own, every day, the words of the disciples when they asked Jesus: "Lord, teach us to pray" (Lk 11:1).

In this year we are invited to become more humble and to leave space for the prayer that flows from the Holy Spirit. It is he who knows how to put into our hearts and onto our lips the right words so that we will be heard by the Father. Prayer in the Holy Spirit is what unites us with Jesus and allows us to adhere to the will of the Father. The Spirit is the interior Teacher who indicates the way to follow. Thanks to him the prayer of even just one person can become the prayer of the entire Church, and vice versa. There is nothing like prayer according to the Spirit to make Christians feel united as the one family of God. It is God who knows how to recognize everyone's needs and how to make those needs become the invocation and intercession of all.

I am certain that bishops, priests, deacons, and catechists will find more effective ways this year of placing prayer as the basis of the announcement of hope which the 2025 Jubilee intends to make resonate in this troubled time. For this reason, the contribution of consecrated persons will be of great value, particularly communities of contemplative life. I hope that in all the shrines of the world, privileged places for prayer, initiatives should be increased so that every pilgrim can find an oasis of serenity and return with a heart filled with consolation. May prayer, both personal and communal, be unceasing, without interruption, according to the will of the Lord Jesus (see Lk 18:1), so that the kingdom of God may spread, and the Gospel reach every person seeking love and forgiveness.

As an aid for this Year of Prayer, some short texts have been produced which, with their simple language, will make possible entry into the various dimensions of prayer. I thank the authors for their contribution and willingly place into your hands these "notes" so that everyone can rediscover the beauty of trusting in the Lord with humility and joy. And don't forget to pray also for me.

Vatican City
September 27, 2023

Franciscus

*For the children we all are, that we may stand
upright and trustingly with Mary.*

For all mothers, of the flesh and of the spirit.

*For all fathers, that they may be both
mothers and fathers.*

Introduction

———

Behold your son …

Rome, April 2003. A young woman called Alexandra, Catholic but non-practicing, was wandering near the church of Tre Fontane. She felt anxious and stressed; her second husband's ex-wife was after her, wanting to harm her. On top of that, her second husband's young son was in difficulties. It was in this troubled state that she came to a little grotto, well away from the normal tourist routes, where Mary had appeared around 1947 to an anticlerical Communist called Bruno Cornacchiola. The place looked ill-cared-for and neglected, with candles that had burnt themselves out, and withered flowers lying around on the floor. In this shrine Alexandra stopped in front of the statue of the Virgin Mary. They looked at each other in silence. Suddenly, she saw that Mary's arm was moving, pointing somewhere. She rubbed her eyes to make sure she wasn't dreaming. No, Mary was pointing at something. She looked to see what it was, and saw a picture of Mary holding the Child Jesus, aged three or four, by the hand. Alexandra instantly understood the message: Mary was asking her to look after Johanne, her second husband's son, who was also four years old. From the depths of her being Alexandra shouted: "NO! That's beyond my strength! The answer is No!" She left the shrine in a state of revolt and rage. Several weeks and several journeys later, Alexandra realized that she had, almost without conscious intention, made a home for the little boy with her own son. All her resistance had melted away, and from then on she did not have just one son but two. Twenty years on, Johanne is still a difficult character. He has settled on another continent, not far from Alexandra. And every time he meets serious problems, he calls his "mother," Alexandra, saying, "You're a mother to me, a real mother, you're my mother." Alexandra recognizes that each time she goes to the support of her second "son," she feels the presence of Mary saying to her yet again, "Look after this child as if he were your own," and she experiences in that instant all of Mary's strength and gentleness. When we cannot manage on our own, someone else often comes to seek us out. In Alexandra's vulnerability it was Mary who came to give her courage and confidence. Johanne has become her son for all eternity.

It was in that place, now known as the Shrine of Our Lady of Revelation, that Mary appeared to Bruno Cornacchiola several times asking him to build a church there. What she said to him was: "People will come to pray here who are lost, parched with thirst. Here they will find love, understanding, and consolation: the true meaning of life. Here in this place, in the grotto where I have appeared several times, there will be a door called the 'Door of Peace'. Everyone must enter by this door."

With Alexandra, we have chosen to enter by this "door" to write about praying with Mary.

When Mary appears, anywhere in the whole world, the places where she appears have points in common with the biblical places where she stayed and lived. In the first chapter we will review these places, asking ourselves what they reveal to us about Mary's identity, and what the inner spaces are that Mary asks us to dwell in today. In the second chapter, we will listen to the very few actual words of Mary given to us in the Gospels, and will look at her gestures, her attitudes, and her eyes, trying to understand their meaning. In other words, to discover where and how she is teaching us to react to people and events. And, finally, in the third chapter, we will ask two holy women about the unique relationship they each had with Mary. The whole piece will be interspersed with phrases from the traditional Orthodox prayer known as the Akathist Hymn. This will lead us toward a new, deep revelation of Mary's closeness to each of us. Here is an extract from it:

Rejoice, place of God's goodwill towards sinners!
Rejoice, our assurance in God's presence!
Rejoice, you who lead us, in silence, to trust!

Geographical and Spiritual Locations

———

On beginning this chapter we need to bear in mind the different levels of understanding we get drawn into when we read, listen to, or watch events from the Bible linked to our own everyday situations. To get an inner grasp on Mary's life we will need to pass on from the visible to the invisible, from what is written to what is implied, in order to let ourselves be taught, become more intelligent, read within and beyond the written words. Jewish tradition offers us a key to reading known as "paradise" or, in Hebrew, "*Pardes*." The four consonants of this word, *pe, reish, daleth, sameck* — p, r, d, and s — form an acronym: They are the initial letters of the Hebrew words for four levels of reading which can be applied to our way of reading, understanding, and grasping what Mary wants to pass on to us.

The first level is literal reading or listening, that is the plain sense of the written or spoken words. The second level invites us to read or listen to something by way of allusion, suggestion, reference, or evocation. The third level is that of interpretation, or enlightenment, of discovery. And the fourth is the revelation of the mystery, seeing. God's word constantly uses these four levels to lead us on a journey *into*, from the external or physical world into the world within. For example, the word *door*. A door is a (normally wooden) object that opens and shuts. That's the first level. A door separates two spaces, it allows or prevents entry, and it also means the attitude of being open or shut. That's the second level. When someone speaks of the door of the heart, it isn't a material object but one of a different order. This verse throws light on it: "Behold, I stand at the door and knock. If anyone hears my voice and opens the door, I will come in to him and eat with him, and he with me" (Rv 3:20). This is the third level. And finally, Jesus says of himself that he IS the door: "Truly, truly, I say to you, I am the door of the sheep. I am the door. If anyone enters by me, he will be saved" (Jn 10:7, 9). This is the fourth level of reading: the revelation of the mystery. In the same way, when Mary, in the Shrine of Our Lady of Revelation in Rome, told Bruno Cornacchiola that people needed to enter by the "Door of Peace," she shows us that she is herself this Door of Peace, which we need to go through.

Where are you, Mary? Where do you dwell?
"Where are you?" This can be the first question we ask when we telephone someone we know, "Where are you?" In what place? In what space? In what setting? It seems a perfectly ordinary question, with no special

significance. Yet we don't talk in the same way when we are on a train as when we're in a quiet room, or in a shop, or in a family gathering. Generally speaking, the physical place where we find ourselves influences the way we take part in a conversation. It's difficult sharing a problem in a supermarket while standing in a queue. The question "Where …?" sets off a dialogue and a coming together; although it appears to be simply about location, it leads to another dimension.

"Where are you?" In the Bible too, it is the first question by God: "the LORD God called to the man and said to him, 'Where are you?' ANd he said … 'I was afraid … and I hid myself'" (Gn 3:9–10). Now, God knew where Adam was. The question "Where are you?" surprises us and makes us think. Is it just a question about physical location? No; God's simple, even naive-sounding question is supposed to make Adam (and therefore us, too) jump, to make us realize that we are no longer at ease in our relationship with him. In other words, the question could be rephrased as: "Are you in the right place? Are you in your place?" If God asks this question, it's meant to stir us up. Whenever he asks a question like that, he's not expecting the person to show him or tell him something he didn't know before. On the contrary, the Lord is challenging us to think, inviting us, and hoping for a meeting, an encounter. In other words, the Lord is asking us, "Where are you at, on the inside?" or even, as St. Augustine explained, "Where are you? I am within you, but I cannot find you there, you're always on your way somewhere else." How should we understand this challenge? Doesn't it refer us back to the "meaning" of our existence, or even to our inmost identity? To the inner place where we are called to meet God? To what makes meaning, that is our way of receiving, welcoming, coming back to God's presence? Are we not, on the inside, a whole inner "universe?" Isn't it our vocation to enter it, inhabit it, and live there? Isn't every place and every space like an "inner matrix," which lays the foundations for what we become in the Lord?

"Where are you, Mary?" We can put this question to the mother of Jesus in the Gospel: "Where are you, Mary?" The physical places where Mary lived or stayed actually matter. There is a link between Mary's identity and the places where she lived. If the Evangelists underlined these places, it's because they wanted to tell us something. That's why this booklet starts by looking at the regions and towns where Mary lived. By doing this we can get closer to her. Little by little she will reveal to us the various spiritual meanings of these places, and allow us to build a closer, more lively relationship with her.

Mary says very little in the Gospels. We hear very few of her words, no confidences, no pleas. We hear direct speech from her just seven times, and we'll get to look at those later on. That's why the places where the Bible shows us Mary living are the first thing we will look at in this prayerful study. The places where she found herself, where she settled, where she set out from, can also speak to us. Because those regions, towns, and villages are also *words*, and hold a meaning for us. When we meet someone for the first time we often ask them where they are from, where they live. Where they live is almost as much a part of their identity as their name.

> *Rejoice, fair land of faith where*
> *the Promise is fulfilled!*
> *Rejoice, land flowing with milk and honey!*

—∞∞—

At Bethlehem in Judea

To understand the different meanings of the various names of biblical places we need to see them in the context of other Scripture passages. The story of Jesus' birth unfolds in a location that has a lot of history: Matthew and Luke tell us it was Bethlehem. Mary and Joseph lived in Nazareth, in the north of Israel, but Jesus was born in the south. Why did they travel to the other end of the country when Mary was pregnant? Jesus was born in Bethlehem because it was there that his parents registered for the census. "And all went to be registered, each to his own town" (Lk 2:3). This short verse shows us that Joseph considered himself a native of Bethlehem, even though he wasn't living there. The Gospel passage explicitly underlines his link to Bethlehem: "And Joseph also went up from Galilee, from the town of Nazareth, to Judea, to the city of David, which is called Bethlehem, because he was of the house and lineage of David, to be registered with Mary, his betrothed, who was with child" (Lk 2:4–5).

Bethlehem was a notable place in biblical geography, being mentioned quite often in the Old Testament. It was the burial place of Jacob's wife Rachel, who had given birth to Benjamin — son of the right, or favorite son (see Gn 35:16–20). It was the home town of Boaz, the husband of Ruth (Ru 1—4) who gave birth to Obed, whose son was Jesse, the father of David. So it was the native town of David (1 Sm 16:1), the shepherd boy whose name means "beloved." It was also named as the place where David's successor, the Messiah, was going to be born, as announced by the prophet Micah: "But you, O Bethlehem Ephrathah, / who are too little to be among the clans of Judah, / from you shall come forth for me one who is to be ruler in Israel" (Mi 5:2). This little town, also called Ephrathah, meaning "fertile," is the place where Mary gave birth to Jesus.

So Bethlehem was where sons were born: Benjamin, favorite, and David, beloved; Bethlehem, then, is a place of birth, filiation, descendence. The Hebrew name "Bethlehem" is an evocative one. *Beth* in Hebrew means, among other things, "house." Its initial letter is also the letter that begins the Old Testament. The Hebrew for "In the beginning" (Gn 1:1) is *Bereshit*, and the first syllable, *be*, can mean "beginning," "house," "grain," "wheat," or "son." If we connect *Bereshit* and

Bethlehem, we can conjecture that Jesus' birthplace is the place of the beginning of an origin, of a filiation, and of a descendence. In this house, *Beth*, the Son is received, and if the Son is received that means there is a Father. Jesus is at once the Son of the Father, the Word and the Bread of Life. *Beth-Lehem* literally means "house of bread."

What does Mary teach us at Bethlehem? That for everyone, Bethlehem is our own birthplace and the place of our beginnings, our origins. There she gives birth to the Son of the Father, she who has been in the Breath of the Father from the beginning. She is the house of the Son, because she contains him, she carries him. And in that sense we also become the house of God. She teaches us to become the dwelling place and receptacle to bring the Word to birth in our turn. Or, in Meister Eckhart's words, she teaches us about the birth of God in our soul. Like her, we, men and women, carry the infant Jesus within us. What's more, we are carried by her in her womb. She is the one who gives birth to us into God's life, as she did for Jesus.

Living at Bethlehem with Mary means living in the knowledge and trust of the Father, in his total, full knowledge, and not under the knowledge of human beings, who will pursue her so that she has to flee from Bethlehem. Mary lived her whole life with people who mostly did not see or understand or acknowledge her. None of us wants to or can live without the acknowledgment, encouragement, and support of those closest to us. Learning about this from Mary is a long journey.

Rejoice, healing of my body!
Rejoice, salvation of my soul!

⸺◦◦◦⸺

Galilee, "crossroads of the nations"

"… a town in Galilee …" Traveling in the Gospels means, especially, walking in Galilee, which is mentioned over fifty times, whereas Judaea is mentioned only about thirty times. Situated in the north of Israel, mountainous and green, it is watered by the River Jordan, with Lake Tiberias forming part of its border. In Mary's time, the people there were fishermen, herdsmen, vine-growers, and growers of olivetrees, fruit trees, and cereal crops. The region of Galilee was calmer than Jerusalem, and subject, like Judaea and Samaria, to the rule of Rome. For the Chosen People who were proud to live in Judaea, Galilee was merely on the margins of the promised land, up in the north, in the region that the prophet Isaiah mentioned (see Is 9:1). It was called "Galilee of the nations" because of its link with the diaspora. Galilee was often looked down on by the inhabitants of Jerusalem.

Living in Galilee means living in a place of constant coming and going, of mixed blood, of diversity, where nothing lasts permanently. It is a place where difference is experienced simply, accepted, and welcomed. It is the region of fresh starts and new beginnings, where everything is still to be received and built, far from the opinions and judgments of the powerful men in Jerusalem. What is this existential "Galilee" that we are invited to return to (Mk 16:7)? A place where diversity and encounter are essential? Is it an inner place, far from worldly or superficial pressures? Isn't it also the space of beginnings and inner calls, when we begin to set off on our journey? What is the "Galilee of our heart" where Mary is waiting for us?

In the region of Galilee, three small towns recur in the Gospel accounts: Capernaum, Cana, and Nazareth. We will visit the latter two, starting with Nazareth, a despised, unknown little town that figures abundantly in spiritual writings, whether in the Cistercian tradition, for example, or in advice by spiritual guides to "live in Nazareth." What are they talking about? How does this "Nazareth" connect with us? And, most of all, why should we go and live there? What exactly does this recommendation mean?

> *Rejoice, you who prepare the Hope of*
> *the journeying nation!*
> *Rejoice, you in whom the whole universe*
> *is reconciled!*

―❧❧❧―

At Nazareth in Galilee

Nazareth is where Jesus spent his childhood and youth, with Mary and Joseph. At the moment of the

Annunciation Mary and Joseph lived in Nazareth, though we don't know how long either of them had been there (see Lk 1:26; Lk 2:4; and Lk 2:39). When they returned from their flight into Egypt, Joseph took his family there (Mt 2:23). Jesus grew up there and spent a large part of his life there (Mt 4:13; Mk 1:9; Lk 2:51; Lk 4:16). The town is only named nine times in the Bible. It is not mentioned at all in the Old Testament — Nazareth does not appear in any of the prophecies, or the historical books, or the psalms. It was an unknown place, where nothing happened, and which left no mark. (Very often, apparitions of Our Lady take place in little townships lost in the mountains or the countryside: Fátima, La Salette, Tepeyac, Champion, Igrista, and many more.) Nazareth was an unknown village, hidden and insignificant. It even had a bad reputation, as John the Evangelist shows. When Philip told Nathanael that Jesus was the Messiah and that he came from Nazareth, Nathanael replied scornfully: "From Nazareth? Can anything good come from that place?" (Jn 1:46). Nazareth marks the hidden life of Mary with Joseph and Jesus.

Nazareth is where Mary hears the words of the angel Gabriel, and where we hear her voice and her words for the first time. For us, living at Nazareth can mean coming to a space where we can at last let ourselves be reached, questioned, and challenged by Mary's voice; a place of reassurance. Nazareth is therefore the place where the eyes of others count for nothing, and where the Word can spring up freely and be heard. The living word demands a background of silence, if it is to escape the closed, empty circle of repetitions. To understand this call we need to be withdrawn and hidden, because sometimes we too are the target of persecution or contempt. Nazareth is a place of freedom, of being liberated from formalism and from social, religious, and other restrictions. Living in Nazareth means being hidden from men's eyes and their illusions, living in the reality of an ordinary daily life bathed in the presence of a mother who brings us up and makes us grow in the spiritual life. Nazareth is the place of restored intimacy with Jesus, with his Father and our Father, in the Spirit-Breath. Living at Nazareth is necessarily living happy, freed from the fear of other people's eyes and their judgments. Nazareth is the place of intimacy and trust, the place of respect and living together fraternally, the place of simplicity and humility. Mary is waiting for us there for our growth and fruitfulness in God. She wants to give birth to us there and make us be reborn.

Rejoice, for before you subtle spirits become hesitant!
Rejoice, for before you the closest reasoning falls apart!

〜◈〜

At Cana in Galilee

"On the third day there was a wedding at Cana in

Galilee, and the mother of Jesus was there" (Jn 2:1). John the Evangelist only writes about Mary twice: once here, at Cana in Galilee, and the other time at the foot of the cross. It is a very special episode because in Matthew's and Luke's Gospels Mary only appears in the accounts of Jesus' birth and childhood. No other Evangelist tells us about the miracle at Cana. At Cana, Jesus and Mary were invited to the wedding. It was a party, with dancing, laughter, and joy. It was a happy, noisy occasion with plenty of conversations, plenty of food, and not enough wine. What does Mary teach us and pass on to us at Cana?

The opening phrase of this short biblical passage, "on the third day," introduces us into another dimension: something exceptional is going to happen. In the Old Testament, "the third day" is a special formula, pointing to the day of the Lord's revelation on Mount Sinai. "Let them … be ready for the third day. For on the third day the LORD will come down on Mount Sinai in the sight of all the people" (Ex 19:11). It announces a manifestation of God. In the New Testament "the third day" is the day of the Resurrection. For example, in the First Letter to the Corinthians, "Christ … was raised on the third day in accordance with the Scriptures" (1 Cor 15:3–4). What is about to happen at Cana, then, is presented as a revelation event, a manifestation that is not human but divine:

When the wine ran out, the mother of Jesus said to him, "They have no wine." And Jesus said to her, "Woman, what does this have to do with me? My hour has not yet come." His mother said to the servants, "Do whatever he tells you." (John 2:3–4)

It is Mary who notices the problem and shares it with her son. And she adds, to the servants, "Do whatever he tells you." Mary's instruction to the servants shows her unconditional trust in Jesus. Mary was the first to open the way, and now she becomes the first to show us the way. Mary, mother of Jesus, sees what the others haven't seen. She doesn't ask Jesus for anything, just shows him the problem. And Jesus seems to answer something else. Mary realizes that Jesus has understood and promptly goes and brings the servants to listen to her son. Despite appearances, Mary and Jesus understand one another, even though we hear his surprising reply, "Woman, what does this have to do with me? My hour has not yet come." The first part of this response does not imply any sort of contempt or disrespect towards Mary, but introduces distance. This is clear from the second part: "My hour has not yet come." This was the "hour" of his passion and death on the cross, which announces the revelation of his resurrection. That is why Jesus sets his Mother at a distance, because the time for beginning his passion has not yet come:

Jesus said to the servants, "Fill the jars with water." And they filled them up to the brim. And he said to them, "Now draw some out and take it to the master of the feast." So they took it. When the master of the feast tasted the water now become wine, and did not know where it came from (though the servants who had drawn the water knew). (John 2:7–9)

In the Bible wine holds a nuptial meaning. In the Song of Songs wine symbolizes love. At the Last Supper Jesus will speak of himself as the True Vine (see Jn 15:1–8). Here, at the wedding feast at Cana, the wine prefigures his love and his perfect gift of himself. It is Jesus who gives himself. By changing the water into wine, it is his own life that Christ is giving to the guests to drink. What is more, Jesus does not want to do it all on his own. Each of the commands spoken by Jesus is carried out straightaway, and Jesus associates the servants with his miracle. This way of acting shows Jesus' desire to make each of us sharers with him. Through Mary and thanks to her, Christ's word calls the servants to cooperate with him to produce this sign, this miracle: turning the water into wine.

Let's think about our "inner Cana." Why do we go to this wedding feast? Because it is a place of shared joy. Being at Cana means being in a space of giving, of gift, because every time we offer a service to someone we are giving ourselves in an act of generosity and light. Service as a gift of self is a transformational act, a testimony of kindness and light. This inner transformation belongs to the order of marriage: Mary not only gives birth to us into divine life, but she also prepares in us our marriage with the Word, her son. Cana is the place of a charity that is not produced by our capabilities but comes from a look received from Mary for us and for our sisters and brothers. In our "inner Cana," Mary comes to change the way we look at everyday things. She shows us the needs of our sisters and brothers, to refer them interiorly to Jesus. Cana is a practical lesson in charity in total humility: doing nothing on our own, but opening ourselves in order to become good wine for our sisters and brothers in Christ's hands. This role is a very active one, because it will mean we have to be right there in everyday places, to let this miracle be worked in us and through us, from the abundance of Jesus' life. That is where our joy is, that is where the true wedding-feast is, that is the sign of an alliance formed by sharing, cooperating, and communion. As Nazareth is the place of growing in God, Cana is the place of charity, through Mary with Jesus.

Rejoice, Servant at the feast where
we share in heavenly things!
Rejoice, spring of water welling
up to eternal Life!

Every life is an inner pilgrimage. On the way we need stopping places where we can receive the repose and peace necessary to enter into the mystery of our becoming in God. Whether it is Bethlehem, Nazareth, Cana, or Galilee, all these places show us transformations to be undertaken: receiving and welcoming our origin and filiation at Bethlehem, resisting the enticements of the world at Nazareth, letting ourselves be astounded and transformed by the eternal wedding feast at Cana, without forgetting to stay in the Galilee that enables us to be constantly open to difference.

Mary's Words

———

Before beginning to read this chapter you are invited to perform a simple exercise. Get inside yourself and try to bring to mind the words that put you in contact with the deepest part of your being, in gentle peace and tranquility. It may be, for example, the name of the person you love most, or perhaps a word that reaches and touches you, and goes with you into an inner space that is calm and full of light. For instance, "consolation," or "garden," or "tenderness," or so many others. Take the time to focus on these "spark" words that bring you light and warmth, that belong to you personally. This exercise enables us to grasp the extent to which certain words support and structure us interiorly and spiritually.

In this second chapter we are going to listen to Mary's words and silences at particular moments. We are going to try and understand how she carries the Word, and how she can help us to enter into our true words, those that restore our intimacy with God the Father, with his Son in the Holy Spirit.

We hear Mary's voice so little in the Gospels: She only spoke seven phrases. Together with the accompanying actions, they reveal her attitudes and inner dispositions. It is up to us to hear them and take them in with the ears of our heart, storing them up in the depths of our heart as she did herself: "But Mary treasured up all these things, pondering them in her heart" (Lk 2:19); or, in another translation, "Mary kept all these things, pondering on them in her heart."

Mary's attitude is the opposite of the one described in the story of the fall of Adam and Eve (see Gn 3:2–7). The consequences of original sin involve three attitudes: first, prioritizing externals, such as distraction, looking around, and dissipation; then, fearing God and considering him as a rival, a judge, or, worse still, an adversary; and, finally, forgetting what we are, where we come from and where we are going, insofar as we forget love, discarding it as a mere illusion. Whereas Mary, with her silences, her adaptability, and her words, teaches us how to adopt a completely different attitude: prioritizing interiority, trusting our Father God, and, finally, keeping his blessings vividly in mind.

*Rejoice, you who sum up the riches
of God's Word!*

How can this come about?

This is the first word said by Mary in the Gospel according to Saint Luke, in reply to the annunciation of the angel. "How will this come about, since I know not man?" or even, "How will this be, since I am a virgin?" (Lk 1:34).

Let's reread the whole passage:

In the sixth month the angel Gabriel was sent from God to a city of Galilee named Nazareth, to a virgin betrothed to a man whose name was Joseph, of the house of David. And the virgin's name was Mary. And he came to her and said, "Greetings, O highly favored one, the Lord is with you!" But she was greatly troubled at the saying, and tried to discern what sort of greeting this might be. And the angel said to her, "Do not be afraid, Mary, for you have found favor with God. And behold, you will conceive in your womb and bear a son, and you shall call his name Jesus. He will be great and will be called the Son of the Most High. And the Lord God will give to him the throne of his father David, and he will reign over the house of Jacob for ever, and of his kingdom there will be no end."

And Mary said to the angel, "How will this be, since I am a virgin?"

And the angel answered her, "The Holy Spirit will come upon you, and the power of the Most High will overshadow you; therefore the child to be born will be called holy — the Son of God. "Behold, I am the servant of the Lord; let it be to me according to your word." And the angel departed from her. (Luke 1:26–35; 38)

Luke says specifically that the angel Gabriel was sent to a *Parthenos*, the Greek term for an unmarried virgin. If she became pregnant through the power of the Holy Spirit, without being married, Mary would immediately be in danger of death — if her fiancé Joseph denounced her and people followed the letter of the Jewish law, she risked being stoned. She was free to refuse this incomprehensible, totally unreasonable event. She found herself in a situation of paradoxical weakness, disorientated by the angel's words, not knowing where they may take her, because they uprooted her from any kind of "normality." The call the Lord addressed to her was bewildering, knocking her off balance instead of reassuring her. In consenting to these events, then, Mary enabled a scandalous situation to turn into grace and the Lord's path. In this way Mary united herself to all the women who have to grapple with complicated, potentially scandalous situations, to show that the Lord is there together with them. She thus proposes a reversal of appearances. Something that in the eyes of everyone seemed like a reason for shame and condemnation — the fact that it was not the time for her to be pregnant, and her promised husband was not the father of her unborn child — was to become a reason for a radical renewal of life.

However, by receiving a visit from an angel of God,

Mary also received a privilege reserved to very few people in the Bible. Origen, the third-century theologian, tells us that the Greek word *kecharitōměnē*, rendered in English as "full of grace," is only used once in the whole of Scripture. So what happened to Mary was exceptional, in fact, unique. After her initial bewilderment, Mary questioned herself, wondering where this greeting could come from and what it meant. For God, thanks to the annunciation by the angel Gabriel, human beings are partners in dialogue — people whose consent needs to be obtained. By agreeing to what the angel told her, she not only showed that she was working with God, but also showed her trust and immense courage in facing the risks involved. In announcing to her the name that she was to give her son, the angel revealed the name of God the Father, because her son is called the "Son of the Most High." Others — Moses, Jacob — had asked to know more. Mary alone received a plain answer.

This visit by the angel to Mary shows us a woman whom God respects. That is why, with a boldness full of respect, she doesn't hesitate to raise an objection. When the angel announces all these things to her, Mary responds with a question: "How will this come about, since I know not man?" She takes her place in the biblical tradition of the patriarchs who argue directly, clearly, and firmly, like Abraham outside Sodom, or Jacob in his combat, or even Moses before the burning bush. Her vigorous forcefulness is that of a patriarch;

she does not abandon the use of reason, and does not trust blindly. In a way, she "confronts" the angel with her question "How?" She doesn't ask "Why?" Most of us, faced with an unexpected happening, whether it is a promotion or a failure, a bereavement or an illness, ask ourselves, "Why is this happening, this surprise, this drama?" "Why him and not me?" and so on. Mary does not ask the angel Gabriel, "Why me?" She receives and takes in his words, her reaction being neither fear nor subservience. She positions herself in a setting of trust and dialogue, and not one of passive resignation or submission. Her "How?" is that of a woman standing on her own feet, neither submissive nor resentful. She wants to cooperate, construct, and communicate, as between two equals. When we ourselves begin to say "How?" to a proposition, we are already engaging ourselves to adopt what is being proposed or adjust to it. Several years ago a married man with a family died quite suddenly, just there in front of them. He had seven children. We acted quickly to support his wife and children in their loss. One of his daughters, aged fifteen, said: "There's no point in wondering why that happened to him, or why it has happened to us. But *how* are we going to live through this tragedy?"

So the first of Mary's "words" doesn't present us with a woman who is self-effacing, or timid, or merely resigned. Her question has nothing sugary or passive about it. It's the question of a woman who is intelligent, open and receptive, neither suppressed nor hesitant nor deceptive. In this first word, Mary speaks to us: "*How* are you going to take in my words? Into what inner attitudes? Where does it find you when someone asks you 'How?' and not 'Why?'"

When we are trying to find our vocation according to Our Lord's wishes, do we ask him, with Mary, "How will this be done?" Like Mary, we can put all our questions to Our Lord, as long as they are asked in the trust that is born of love, and not demandingly or as though stating a claim. Our Lord prefers us to question him lovingly rather than stay silent in false resignation. We can confront Our Lord, as Mary did, just as Abraham argued with God to save the few just men in Sodom and Gomorrah. It's an ardent dialogue, not from a position of pride and opposition, but holding an exchange with the Lord our God, standing simply and humbly by his side.

Rejoice, harbor of peace for those tossed
on the stormy waves of this life!
Rejoice, plank of salvation for those who aspire
to the fullness of life!

⸻

Let what you have said be done to me
After listening to Mary's "How?" we can now go on to her second "word," which concludes the Gospel account: "Behold, I am the servant of the Lord; let it be

to me according to your word" (Lk 1:38). She gives her consent, saying yes unreservedly and unconditionally to God's call. It is important for us to try and hear this word of Mary's at each of the tough situations she is faced with: First of all in Nazareth, facing the hostility of the people who take her son for a madman; then during the various unjust tortures inflicted on Jesus; and again at the foot of the cross when her son breathes his last. Each time, Mary says that brief phrase again: "Let what you have said be done to me." In that answer of hers, she gives us to understand her total, definitive trust. She overcomes her weakness by relying on God's relationship with her — that is why she receives, consents, and accepts it all with her whole mind and will. Her trust is a decided choice, without passivity or subservience; a choice for what God wants and for how he acts. Her trust is not based on her own abilities; like Peter, she will walk resolutely on the water, and do so her whole life long. In each event and situation she is upheld by her unshakable trust, expressed aloud on the day of the Annunciation. She will live her life in such a way that neither misunderstanding nor rejection nor suffering can get the better of the unconditional dynamic of her being towards God. She puts herself at the service of the future life, the life to come, ready to follow whatever winding path God may point her to.

As for us, our trust is still full of questioning and sometimes refusal. That realization is not a tragedy, but rather a call for us to go forward. Mary teaches us to base our life not on our own generosity but on trust. Too often, we want to give, and to give what doesn't belong to us — our life, our time, our things — while what is really being asked of us is to trust. Dwelling in our "house of trust" will produce in us a way of giving that will not follow our own criteria alone. This place of trust in us is the support, security, and foundation that enables us to go forward in a new way, one that has nothing to do with cultural or worldly criteria. It is then that defenses give way, resistance vanishes before the proof that there is an impossibility to be lived through: It is impossible to sustain and hold onto our life with our own strength alone, relying only on ourselves.

Mary's trust reposes on God's trust in her. That trust is the strength and power that sustain her; God's trust dwells within her. Like the word Jesus will say to Peter, "Take heart; it is I. Do not be afraid" (Mt 14:27), this word comes not as a result of counting on our own strength, not by calculating, not by measuring our own abilities, but by giving ourselves up in an act of radical trust to God's word. Mary does that, and her act is like a kind of detachment and death. Having accepted the revelation of what was impossible for her, Mary sees strength and freedom coming to birth within her. Mary's consent is the sign of her freedom, her liberation. She is liberated from fear, from the desire for control, from the fear of the unknown. When we cross over the threshold of radical trust, a much greater freedom is offered: that of being able to direct our will to what is essential, that of being able to live out our time with great effectiveness, and being present to ourselves and to other people. The desire to defend ourselves against having anything taken away, and the need to control and dominate over others, gradually fade and vanish away. And, at peace, we can say with Mary: Lord, "Let what you have said be done to us."

Rejoice, you in whom exhausted spirits are reborn!
Rejoice, for in you those who are wounded by their past
find strength!

―――⟨∂/∂/∂⟩―――

Why have you done this to us?
Saint Luke is the only Evangelist who gives us an account of Jesus' childhood. Here he tells the episode of the Finding in the Temple (see Lk 2:41–52), designating the action of finding what was lost. Jesus was twelve when he went to the Temple in Jerusalem with his parents to celebrate the Passover, one of the greatest Jewish feasts. In his account Luke lets us share in the reactions and emotions of Mary and Joseph. The whole episode has the flavor of a testimony, inviting us into the heart of their mutual relationship. Their reaction was surprising; after searching for Jesus for three days, their first reaction was not one of reproach, but

the mute admiration of a mother and father on seeing their son's precocity amidst a group of learned men.

> After three days they found him in the temple, sitting among the teachers, listening to them and asking them questions. And all who heard him were amazed at his understanding and his answers. And when his parents saw him, they were astonished. (Luke 2:46–48)

After the admiration and astonishment come their legitimate reproaches. Mary does not scold him directly, but makes him a motherly remonstrance. She calls him "my child," and shares with him the pain and anguish of those three days spent looking for him:

> And his mother said to him, "Son, why have you treated us so? Behold, your father and I have been searching for you in great distress." And he said to them, "Why were you looking for me? Did you not know that I must be in my Father's house?" (Luke 2:48–49)

This question is one that plenty of fathers and mothers have put to their children. It is a completely justifiable one, and is neither judgmental nor condemnatory. Mary is responsible for her son, Jesus, and here she begins to practice a special kind of detachment. She can no longer hold onto her son, or hold him back. After three days' tormented search, Mary is called to take on something totally new, something that belongs to the order of mystery: "Behold, I am making all things new" (Rv 21:5). Without any warning, this event produces in Mary a surprise, even a kind of unbalancing or reframing. Her question is that of a mother who is prepared to let herself be led elsewhere, anywhere. It also comes in the Psalms: "Why, O LORD, do you stand afar away? / Why do you hide yourself in times of trouble?" (Ps 10:1). Mary is summoned to live the present moment with all its surprises and unforeseen elements. Nothing in life is ever fixed, whether in our ordinary lives or in life with Our Lord: There are times of withdrawal and uncertainty, and likewise times of great presence and trusting faith. All this in an unending search and a certain pain when we cannot hold onto what we thought we had found. Mary teaches us to keep trusting even when there is no evidence and no proof. Like her, we have to search without fretting, explore without looking for results, and ask without reproaching.

This family story at Jerusalem is one of the very rare glimpses we have of Jesus between his birth and the age of twelve. Why is his age given? In Jewish tradition, twelve is the age when a boy can start going to study in the religious school known as the yeshiva in the Talmudic tradition. It is also the approximate age for the feast of the bar mitzvah, celebrating adulthood in the Jewish community. Traditionally, in the course of the celebration, the boy reads a passage of the Torah and then answers a certain number of questions, to demonstrate that he knows at least the basics of it. However, in the scene we are considering, the model is reversed: It is not Jesus who learns and answers questions; here Jesus teaches and puts questions to the sages and the doctors of the Law. In other words, Jesus presents himself as a teacher, not a pupil. The first words we hear directly from him are pronounced in the Temple at Jerusalem and concern his relationship with the Father. If the Evangelist chose to record them it is because they contain a challenge and a decisive interpretation: Jesus is not merely a child born of Mary at Bethlehem, he is the Son of God, and God himself. This episode is not a mere anecdote or just an incidental story: Jesus is in his own home with the Father, and the Temple is his house. This twelve-year-old boy calls his parents to adopt an approach of conversion, change, and newness. Once again, it is a question by Mary, his mother, that sets us off, on our road, shakes us off balance and challenges us. This careful, attentive, concerned mother shows closeness, solicitude, and commitment with regard to our path and our calling. In asking us the same question — "Why have you done this?" or rather "Why have you done this to us?" — she makes us understand that nothing of what we experience leaves her indifferent. She is a sharer in each of our escapades or transgressions. Her son's answer is for all of us:k orientation, compass, and meaning.

Rejoice, you in whom man is raised up!
Rejoice, for you unmask the traps of idols!

The angel came into her presence; they found him in the Temple

The words and events we have just followed take place in particular places: the house, the Temple. These are highly symbolic places at the level of building, living, and welcoming. They show us the way in which God is present, if he lives there or not. The normal function of every house is hospitality and welcome; in the Old Testament, the house is a place of openness, rest, and protection. The house is also a space of intimacy. Even today, the door of a house opens inward, not outward, and we enter into this dwelling through a door that opens before us into another place. In the Gospel, the angel came "into Mary's presence," in other words, she received him into her house. Not only is Mary's house the image of a hospitality that receives and welcomes, she makes her own self into a dwelling place for the other.

With Mary, the point of our spiritual life could be summed up as: Who comes into our place? Who visits us? Do we want to be close family members in Mary's "house?" Mary reveals herself to us not through what she has done, but through what God has done in her, because she let herself be visited. That means that by opening the door of our inner "house," we give entry to a presence, the presence of the Holy Spirit, acting, transforming, and vivifying our whole being. Mary, who lives in her house, also teaches us to live with ourselves, not dispersed outward, so that we can grow like a tree up towards the light, or to plunge into the depths of our being and become aware of the incommunicable revelation of the presence of God our Lord. The more we dwell on the inside, within ourselves, the more human we are, incarnate, and able to be united to everyone. Because the closer we are to our God-Love, the closer we are to other people. To inhabit our house, to reconnect with our heart, the place of love and wisdom, to be ceaselessly converted and receive a heart of flesh (see Ez 36:26) — that is one of Mary's lessons for us. Once awakened, our heart becomes capable of loving, because it lets itself be guided by Mary's hand. Love becomes the "place" where we are called to dwell with Mary. Being in our own home in order to be in Mary's home and take her to stay with us means letting ourselves be inhabited and visited by trust in God, by the memory of his gifts and blessings, dwelling on them and making our home there in order to become what we are called to be.

The other significant place where the Child Jesus is found with Mary is the Temple. In the Old Testament the Temple of God was the place where his Name and his Presence dwelt. In this huge space that opened up to his people, they found light, sweet-smelling incense, and the sign of the Covenant. Its whole purpose, always and above all, had to be prayer. It was a basic spiritual orientation, the polestar, for the Jewish people: the dwelling place of God among men. With Jesus, who "dwelt among us" (Jn 1:14), the Temple became "incarnate" and took flesh, in Christ. And in a way, Mary represents the Temple of waiting.

When she found her lost son in the Temple, she revealed to us that temples built of stone pointed us to another presence that dwelt, from that time on, in each of us: "Or do you not know that your body is a temple of the Holy Spirit within you, whom you have from God?" (1 Cor 6:19). With Mary, the sacred space of the Temple takes on another meaning. Finding Jesus in the Temple means finding him within ourselves, living and working through his Spirit-Breath in the everyday setting of streets, shops, and all kinds of scenery, that ordinariness linked to the Presence, being inhabited by God himself.

Rejoice, Temple of the Infinite God!
Rejoice, unbelievable news for unbelievers!
Rejoice, Good News for believers!

Mary treasured all these things and pondered them in her heart. … His mother stored up all these things in her heart

To conclude this chapter about Mary's words in the Gospels, let's choose not a spoken word but an inner attitude. Namely, how did Mary retain the living words that are events? Where did she store them up? Where did she watch over them? And where did she meditate on them?

Mary never takes her stand on cerebral reasoning, or endless mental questioning. She situates herself in her heart, and takes that as her basic position. She is not in her head nor in her emotions: she is in her heart (see 2:19, 51). Having listed the geographical and spiritual places such as Galilee, Nazareth, Cana, Bethlehem, the Temple, or the house, this is where we come to: *the* place, that of the heart, the heart of the heart. The grace that Mary grants all those who travel with her is to go down and return to the heart. That heart that is the place of our deepest identity. The heart that is called "room," "house," or "inner cell" and that fulfills three essential functions: the capacity for silence, awareness, and decisiveness. Inner silence is experienced in prayer and meditation. The capacity for awareness and the spoken word enables us to identify and name inner motions. And finally purpose, decisiveness, sustains our inner dynamism so that we do not let ourselves get distracted by the demands of the world. It was that place, the place of the heart, that Adam lost when the LORD God asked him, "Adam, where are you?" And Adam answered, "I heard your voice and I was afraid, and I hid." Once again Mary teaches us the opposite of that attitude. The things that happened to her — the birth of her son, with the shepherds and the angels as his courtiers, then finding him in the Temple, with his unexpected response — these things did not frighten Mary away; she did not hide when she heard God's voice in these events. No, she stored them up, "guarded" them, meditated on them, retained them, gathered them, and sought their meaning within her heart. What happened in her and around her was always an opportunity for her to return to her heart. If we, like her, "keep" and "guard" these words, we become in our turn the house of God and of his word. "If anyone loves me, he will keep my word, and my Father will love him, and we will come to him and make our home with him" (Jn 14:23).

To meditate is to enter into "paradise," as explained at the start of this booklet. Meditating means, in fact, going through the different levels of reading. First of all, passing through literal, simple (or even simplifying) understanding; then going through the second level, linked to symbol; and thus opening ourselves to the third level, the search that introduces us into light and a new grasp of Scripture, the understanding of the heart; until we reach the last level, that of the secret of God. Mary is the one who teaches us to meditate in order to descend into the secret of the Heart of her son, the Word of God.

Mary teaches us to store up the verse "Did you not know that I must be busy with my Father's affairs?" The first level of reading would be to restrict this verse to what it literally says: that the Child Jesus must occupy himself in the works of his Father. The second level opens up the meaning of his words when we take the time to compare different possible translations: "my Father's affairs," or "things of the Father of me," or again "to be in the house of my Father," or else "it is inevitable that I am there in what belongs to my Father." With these translations, we enter naturally into a new meaning: Jesus is the child of the Father, they are one and the same thing. We penetrate progressively deeper into the concealed heart of this "word": Jesus is declaring that he is the Son of the Father, and that Mary ought to, needs to, discover the meaning of his connection with his Father.

Here we are being asked to situate ourselves within the things of everyday life, and adjust ourselves to them. What are these "affairs" that are so essential? In other words, how do we live our relationships with our family and close friends? Again, where are we in our relational freedom? If everything belongs to God, comes from God, and returns to him, why should we continue to be attached, shackled, or imprisoned by any worldly goal?

Meditating is reading, chewing over, murmuring, ruminating, and reciting the words, gathering them and fixing them in our mind in order to keep them in our heart, and so finally becoming listening and love. Only words and events that are meditated on can bring about new women and men. Meditating does not mean consuming some event or fact, or utilizing it for our own advantage. Meditating in our heart and with our heart means locating ourselves in a place of free giving and gratitude. When Mary meditated and stored up, she received what had just happened, accepted it, and retained it in the sense of remembering it. Not to find a solution, but to inscribe on the memory of her heart what God had done in her. She meditated and kept watch so as not to forget; she meditated and stored up so as to fix in her memory the essence of it all and not be distracted or confused. She meditated on what was happening to her without aiming to grasp it rationally, and in this she teaches us to do the same. With Mary, and as the woman or a man that we are, we are asked to look at our life and question ourselves on "how" to live it.

Why do we find such difficulty in meditating? The resistance we experience exists to impel us to go deeper, it tests us in order to strengthen us for that inner descent. Our resistance has a value, it teaches us to face and overcome any obstacle on our inner path. The Hebrews also managed to cross the Red Sea after overcoming all sorts of doubts and mistrust. Resistance that we have faced and overcome is fruitful; it has a teaching function. After all, meditation is a kind of accomplishment, one that satisfies a need. People who meditate put a stop to their inner agitation, because it turns into prayer and meditation. Their meditative withdrawal gives place to a different way of thinking, of forming concepts, and of living. Meditating means, in a way, joining in with God's Sabbath and entering into his repose, entering deeply into his active grace and withdrawing from the world around us. Meditation makes space, and there comes forth from it an act of true love, which is genuine, not an illusion. Striking roots in meditation in this way means making an act of charity and benevolence, withdrawing so that the Other, and other people, may take their full place in our lives. To meditate is to respond to the Word by turning to our own heart in order to breathe and come back to life and find the place of Love and a wedding feast. Mary points out the way for us.

Mary's words and attitudes are never excuses. She hasn't got to prove anything. Mary keeps and works on her heart, and in doing so becomes a listener to the Holy Spirit. That is why she stands on her own two feet, vertical, straight. With Mary we learn to stand vertically, we learn to dwell in our inner land. Mary lives out the vocation of each of us; to be mothers, and married. A woman is a mother biologically, but both men and women have the vocation to the essential maternity: to bring the Incarnate Word to birth in themselves. It is in us that God's encounter with ourselves is played out, in us that God seeks himself and that his accomplishment is brought about. If we receive and accept, if we espouse God's Word in us, then the light bursts forth. All light is the meeting of an act of emitting with a receptivity, in a perfectly adjusted relationship. Union is achieved in these successive acts of meditation and integration, until God is born in us. Human marriages and human maternity are preparations for giving birth to the God we carry, and for the wedding feast that awaits each of us.

Mary's meditation is practiced in the faith that is in continual tension towards the Father; in the hope that is a certainty that these realities are within us, waiting to be gathered, because hope is linked to the presence of the Son in the Father; and in the charity that unifies because it is the work of God's Spirit.

In the Book of Genesis, God asks Abraham to "cultivate and take care of" his earth in the garden. That's like a definition of meditation. Mary watches over, takes care of, gathers together, and retains the things that happen to her. She does what God asks of Adam, takes care of and watches over what is done for the accomplishment of a promise of life, because God watches over and works on her heart. St. Louis de Montfort compares Mary to a high mountain upon which God has built his dwelling-place, "upon which Jesus teaches and remains for ever, a mountain where we are transfigured with him, where we die with him, where we ascend into heaven with him." And this same saint calls Mary the oratory, the house where God lives, the place where we find him. It is only in this house, it's only in this blessed place, that we will find the remedies we need to grow to adulthood in our vocation.

Rejoice, you lead us towards trust in silence!
Rejoice, you lead believers to intimacy with the Spouse!

Women Saints and Mary

This third chapter transports us to other geographical and spiritual locations. We are going to discover how Mary made herself known and allowed herself to be visited by two holy women. These particular saints were French, but they could equally well have been Spanish, Colombian or Indian. Because Mary is never ruled by outward appearances. She lets herself be seen by whoever she chooses, poor or rich, ignorant or well-educated, anywhere in the world.

St. Catherine Labouré

In nineteenth-century France, a peasant family was in tears. Their forty-two-year-old mother had just died, leaving her three young children orphans. One of them was Catherine, nine years old, also known as Zoe, who couldn't read or write. She decided to choose another mother for herself. When she was alone in the room, still crying, she climbed onto the piece of furniture which had a statue of Our Lady on it, and asked her to take her mother's place. At that moment her tears ceased, and Mary taught her not to cry, but to take charge of her own life. In 1830, when Catherine was twenty-four, she went to start her formation in Paris with the Daughters of Charity founded by St. Vincent de Paul.

Catherine Labouré received and welcomed three apparitions of Mary. They were of decisive importance for the whole Church. The way Mary came to meet Catherine Labouré is a lesson for us. Mary wants to talk to us, too, and visit us. Not in the same way as Catherine Labouré, but she wants to show us a path, point out a route to us, teach us not only to pray but to become prayer, and to give meaning to our prayers.

In July 1830, Catherine was woken up in the night by what seemed to be a child who led her into the chapel. There, after a long wait, Catherine saw Mary, seated in a chair. It was an extraordinary event, and indeed Catherine didn't want to believe it, resisting. When she finally realized it was true, she threw herself into Mary's lap. Mary pointed towards the altar, where Catherine would need to come to receive total consolation. Before that initial apparition, Mary first made Catherine wait. She kept vigil in the chapel for about an hour. That wait served to test her and develop her trust. It enabled her to enter into herself, without wanting to get something she could hold on to. With Mary, it's never everything all at once. Then there came a very quiet sign. As Catherine explained, she heard the rustle of a dress, "the swish of a silk gown," like a gentle breeze. Mary's apparitions often take place discreetly, like a light breath, never with a fanfare of trumpets. Then Mary appeared and sat down in a chair. Catherine tells the story: "I gave one jump and was there with her, kneeling on the altar step, my hands resting on the Blessed Virgin's knees. What I experienced was the sweetest moment of my whole life." Catherine's long wait was rewarded in a way that surpassed anything imaginable. She rested her hands on Our Lady's knees. It was an overwhelming moment of simple, sweet, gentle closeness. Mary let herself be approached and touched, in motherly, loving intimacy. They looked into each other's eyes and talked together for two hours, in the most respectful familiarity. During that first apparition Mary told Catherine that she was to receive "a mission." With motherly foresight and teaching skill, Mary prepared Catherine's heart and dispositions to receive the task that would follow.

Four months later, on November 27, Catherine received her instructions for having the "Miraculous Medal" struck. It had to have these words inscribed on it: "O Mary, conceived without sin, pray for us who have recourse to you." Then Our Lady assured her that "abundant graces will be bestowed upon those who wear it trustingly." Within a few years, a very large number of cures made the medal famous. Forty years later, a billion copies of the Miraculous Medal were in existence. It is one of the best-known representations of the Blessed Virgin Mary in the world.

Understanding Mary means seeing the motherly concern she feels, moment by moment, for every human being. Mary wants to be close to us, and she comes right down into our daily lives. She gives us a simple, easy way to ask her for things: a little medal to wear close to our hearts. She wants everyone to receive her rays of light. Indeed, Catherine said that certain precious stones did not glitter, and she heard Our Lady saying to her, "Those stones that remain in darkness represent the graces that people forget to ask me for."

In her apparitions to St. Catherine Labouré, Mary, by making herself so accessible, sought to banish any kind of fear. She wants everyone to receive the salvation, healing, and liberation brought by her son Jesus. Like every mother, she is well acquainted with her children's defiance, embarrassment, or indifference. Her apparitions to Catherine testify to her luminous strength in associating us closely with herself and making us into true children of the same Father.

Rejoice, unshakable support of our faith!
Rejoice, for you lead believers to Christ!

<hr/>

St. Bernadette of Lourdes

In the first chapter we were in Nazareth, a lost, despised village, and now we come to Lourdes, an isolated, unknown hamlet two centuries ago, when there was a cholera outbreak there.

"Will you do me the favor of coming here every day for a fortnight?" Mary asked Bernadette Soubirous in 1858. Bernadette was 14, just-over-four-and-a-half-feet tall, and she had come to the banks of the River Gave to gather firewood to sell so she could buy some food for her family. Like Jesus, Mary asks questions, and asks for a meeting, without any pressure or constraint. She asks for, and wants, a free, loving relationship, free from any kind of possessiveness. She manifested her presence to Bernadette by a slight noise, "like the wind blowing," and the "lady beckoned her to come closer." Bernadette did not dare to approach; she was extremely frightened and thought she was seeing things. The barefooted lady, who tried to speak to this simple child, managed to calm her down and make friends with her. They ended up by saying the Rosary together, without the Lady "moving her lips, but just passing the rosary beads through her fingers." Mary, "the beautiful lady," appeared to Bernadette eighteen times.

The seventh apparition was undoubtedly the most significant of all. Bernadette recounted:

The lady told me that I had to go and drink from the spring. ... She pointed me to a spot under the rock. I went there and found a little water that looked like mud, so little that I could hardly get any in the palm of my hand. But I obeyed, and started scraping; after that I could get some in my hands. The first three times, the water was so dirty that I threw it away; the fourth time, I was able to drink it.

The true pilgrimage began. Not one that involved going abroad, or traveling for miles, but a true pilgrimage to the spring of water. This spring already existed, but was lost in the great expanse of tumbled rock. Mary brought the spring to life. She does that with each of us. Through means of readings or encounters, Mary awakens that hidden, secret, subterranean presence. Then comes the time when we have to "scrape" at the stones of our inner land. It requires time and careful listening to dig deep into ourselves, to take up the mud of our dark, ill-intentioned, and twisted thoughts and actions. Working the earth of our inner selves in Mary's presence means plunging into dirty, muddy waters, and going back again and again without getting discouraged. Bernadette threw away the muddy water three times before the spring finally began to flow, and she drank some.

In all the Scriptures, the figure three indicates fullness, totality (the three temptations of Jesus, the three days before his resurrection). This pilgrimage to the source of water tests the heart: It brings to light duplicities, betrayals, lies. At the bottom of the "well," after it has been cleared of its stones and mud, a little clear water will begin to flow. It becomes an inner spring of peace, authenticity, and clarity. Mary's teaching skill in leading us along this way is that of a patient, smiling, loving mother.

Today at Lourdes the stream continues to flow, after more than a hundred and fifty years. People come there to pray, kneel, entrust themselves, and bathe in the water of the pools. This water that never ceases to flow is superabundant, like the graces that the mother of Jesus wishes to grant. There are no restrictions, formalities, or permissions needed to drink the water: It's free. Lourdes speaks to the heart, speaks of life with God. In heaven we will all be together, with no distinctions of races or social classes, filled to overflowing with charity and service for everyone, living only for Love. Lourdes is a foretaste of that future life. And it all began with the receptivity of a young girl who allowed Mary to encounter her. In the cradle of the ordinary, there wells up the "extraordinary" of the Lord our God.

The apparitions of Mary to Bernadette tell us how she enters into relationships with us; the way she does so is unique each time, and totally respectful. During the second apparition, Mary smiled at Bernadette and bent down towards her (and therefore towards each of us). Mary did not look towards heaven but towards Bernadette, as if to say that heaven is in the other person. In the subsequent apparitions the beautiful lady spoke in the same dialect as Bernadette, addressing her with respect, and looking at her as a person in her own right. Mary reveals herself in a relationship with others which is the image of herself: clear, attentive, filling the heart with joy and peace. In a unique way, adapted to each individual, she puts herself within everyone's reach.

Rejoice, Rock from which flows the spring
that quenches the thirst of the parched!
Rejoice, Pillar of Fire who light
up our journey through the night!

Conclusion

———

After years of roaming, the prodigal son in the parable (see Lk 15:17) pulled himself together, began to think, found himself again, and "came to his senses," writes the evangelist. Found at last! He was at home. We could add he was at home with Mary. From that place he was able to understand himself and listen, discern, and decide "I will go to my Father."

This booklet is addressed to all those who, like Ulysses or the prodigal son in the parable, are seeking the path to find, or refind, their place, their proper location. It is intended for those who wish to experience a home-coming and a wedding feast in their inner life. It is from there that they will be able to go out and come back, walk confidently, storing up words and events in their memory, and putting them together to find their meaning.

Throughout this booklet the focus has been on places geographical, emotional, interior, and spiritual. The question about place is so vital that it is the very first question God puts to Adam (and therefore to each of us), "Where are you?" It is taken up in the Gospels, this time by Jesus' disciples: Where do you live? Isn't this the question of everyone's life? The question of how to find one's place, to be in the right place, one's rightful place? How should we find that place? Is it attainable?

Jesus, when he was about to die, said some words that Saint John left to us in his Gospel:

> When Jesus saw his mother and the disciple whom he loved standing nearby, he said to his mother, "Woman, behold, your son!" Then he said to the disciple, "Behold, your mother!" And from that hour the disciple took her to his own home. (John 19:26–27)

John took Mary, the mother of Jesus, with him, into his home, following Jesus' words. We, too, have opened the door to Mary, to take her into our home and have her with us. With John the Evangelist we "make a place for her in our home"; thanks to her we find our rightful place day by day. When we do this, her presence reveals itself throughout her words and her journeyings. And she shares with us her own zest for life. Because Mary, mother, sister, and companion, is the one who takes each of us by the hand to lead us towards new lands. The pilgrimages towards which she guides us are called interiority, trust, and memory. She does all this in order to bring the life of the Holy Spirit to birth in us. She leads us inside ourselves, into the depths of our depth, to the kernel of our being, into our hiddenmost dwelling place, into the place of the heart. That is the gift she gives us, because she herself is there, always. She is the heart totally open to grace and the Holy Spirit. That is her identity.

As mother to each of us, Mary reveals to us the path of her place of grace. She prepares this inner path, leads us to it, and sets us upon it. Whether we are farmworkers, officials, doctors, or teachers, the one essential thing in our whole life is to find that place in ourselves, to establish ourselves there in a state of listening, discernment, and decision. Living doesn't just happen automatically, and it isn't an easy thing to do. To live on the surface or scattered about, with no guidance or compass, is exhausting. To walk aimlessly, without finding meaning, is fruitless. To take Mary with us and into our life effects a change in our life and inner location. Secretly, silently, she transforms our resistances and our refusals, overturns our projects, as she did in the case of Alexandra. With indescribable sensitivity of touch she brings us down from our will to dominate and control our own existence. She asks us to live in the space of gift.

Mary prolongs in each of us today the trust that she lived in throughout her life on earth. Her task is to deliver us from our fear of God our Father, to place us in his hands and inscribe us in his intimate life. She leads us to a personal, adult relationship with God. Having God for our Father is first of all having Mary for our mother. Trusting, giving our trust to, or putting our trust in Mary opens us and gives us zest and dynamism. Fear, worry, and despair block, hamper, and diminish our zeal and fervor. Mary's life teaches us that this trust is built in weakness and vulnerability, and structures us with incessant comings and goings, "yesses" and "nos." It makes us recover joy, sweetness, peace, and security.

Where does Mary's memory come from? Her heart is the place of her memory. To be with Mary is to return to the place where memories take on meaning and purpose. Rereading the events of one's life and looking for their meaning opens up new perspectives. For each of us, it is about remembering, carefully storing up the unexpected signs in our daily lives, and putting them together. This remembering, which is like the work of a watchman or lookout, teaches us vigilance, perseverance, and hope. Everything that happens to us makes sense. With Mary, it is up to us to store and watch in order to become instruments ready to serve and carry Jesus. Blessed are those who keep and practice the Word, Jesus tells us; they shall be called "my mother and my brothers" (Lk 8:21).

Is it possible to be reborn today? This question, put to Jesus in the past by the wise and learned Jew Nicodemus, is one we ask today. Is it possible to be reborn in Mary, thanks to her? That is the whole meaning of this booklet. It is about her enabling God to be born in us; and our becoming Jesus' mother to bring him to birth in our relationships. Mary gives birth to this life of God in us; she takes us inside our own hearts, she teaches us to trust, she keeps our memory in the Father's love. With Mary, we become Jesus' mother in the peace of love. Like Alexandra, we, too, will be able to become Jesus' "mother and sisters and brothers" by receiving and welcoming each of the people who are sent to us.

Available at
OSVCatholicBookstore.com
or wherever books are sold

In preparation for the Jubilee Year 2025, the Exploring Prayer series delves into the various dimensions of prayer in the Christian life. These brief, accessible books can help you learn to dialogue with God and rediscover the beauty of trusting in the Lord with humility and joy.

Prayer Today: A Challenge to Overcome
Notes on Prayer: Volume 1
by Angelo Comastri
In order to have saints, what is needed are people of authentic prayer, and authentic prayer is that which inflames with a fire of love. Only in this way is it possible to lift the world and bring it near to the heart of God. To pray in truth, we must present ourselves before God with the open wounds of our smallness and our sin. Only in this way will the encounter with God be an encounter of liberation and redemption.

Praying with the Psalms
Notes on Prayer: Volume 2
by Gianfranco Ravasi
This little guide to the Psalms includes four cardinal points: a general reflection on prayer, the breath of the soul; a panoramic look at the psalmic texts; a portrait of the two protagonists, God and the worshipper, but also the intrusion of the presence of evil; and finally, an anthology of brief commentaries on the Psalms most dear to tradition and the liturgy. The hope is that all the faithful may draw fully from this wonderful treasury of prayers.

The Jesus Prayer
Notes on Prayer: Volume 3
by Juan Lopez Vergara
This book explores the unique experience of the fatherhood of God for Jesus Christ, whom he calls Abba — which in his native Aramaic language means "Dad." Throughout his earthly life, Jesus is in contact dialogue with Abba. From his Baptism in the Jordan through his public ministry and ultimately his crucifixion, this relationship will mark him forever, transforming his life, and our lives, too.

Praying with Saints and Sinners
Notes on Prayer: Volume 4
by Paul Brendan Murray
The saints whose writings on prayer and meditation

are explored in this book are among the most celebrated in the great spiritual tradition. The aim of this book is to discover what help the great saints can offer those of us who desire to make progress in the life of prayer, but who find ourselves being constantly deflected from our purpose, our tentative efforts undermined perhaps most of all by human weakness.

Parables on Prayer
Notes on Prayer: Volume 5
by Anthony Pitta

What characterizes, in a singular way, Jesus's teaching on prayer is the recourse to parables. Jesus did not invent a new system for praying. Jesus was not a hermit, a Buddhist monk, or a yogi. He instead chose the daily life of his people to teach prayer with parables. This book explores the parables in the Gospels explicitly related to prayer. The reader is guided by Jesus, the original teacher of prayer with parables.

The Church in Prayer
Notes on Prayer: Volume 6
by Carthusian Monks

Carthusian Monks reside in several international monasteries. Founded in 1084 by Saint Bruno, the Order of Carthusians are dedicated to prayer, in silence, in community. Like other cloistered religious, the Carthusians live a life focused on prayer and contemplation.

The Prayer of Mary and the Saints
Notes on Prayer: Volume 7
by Catherine Aubin
When Mary appears, anywhere in the whole world, the places where she appears have points in common with the biblical places where she stayed and lived. This book reviews these places, examining what they reveal to us about Mary's identity, and what the inner spaces are that Mary asks us to dwell in today. This book also explores the unique relationship two holy women each had with Mary, leading us toward a new, deep revelation of Mary's closeness to each of us.

The Prayer Jesus Taught Us: The "Our Father"
Notes on Prayer: Volume 8
by Hugh Vanni
This book identifies the theological-biblical structure underlying the Lord's Prayer and situates it in the living environment of the early Church. This will give us a framework of reference, and as a result we will see first the antecedents in Mark, then the systematic presentation of Matthew, Paul's push forward, the accentuation of Luke, and, finally, the mature synthesis found in John.